Two Year Olds -
Not So Terrible
Once You Get to Know Them

Georgia Janisse

Two Year Olds – Not So Terrible Once You Get to Know Them

www.2-isms.com

www.GJanisseArtist.com

Cover art by Georgia Janisse, available at www.pennylanepublishing.com

ISBN 1482376423
ISBN 13: 978-1482376425

Acknowledgments

Special thanks to my first two year olds: my daughters Linda Long, Charity Thayer, Sarah Janisse Brown, and Heather Danielle Evans. They let me see how challenging raising twos can be, and they provided me with lots of two-year-old grandchildren to 'study,' test ideas on, and enjoy. With both quotes and ideas – they are really my co-authors. A specific thank you to my grandson Ryan James Rud. As a two year old he was an intense mix of delight and stubbornness, joy and frustration! He, along with his three cousins of the same age, set me on my quest to understand twos; at thirteen he was an excellent proofreader for this book. Thanks also to my husband of forty-three years, Dennis, who made it all possible in so many ways.

Foreword

After reading my book, Matt (not his real name) may have been thinking: "It can't be this easy. If these things really worked wouldn't everyone be doing it, and two year olds wouldn't act the way they do?!" One of my daughters had given him an advance copy of this book; being the father of a two year old, he immediately read it cover to cover. The next day, as he buckled his little daughter into her car seat, he failed to notice that he had left his map book on the back seat. As he began to drive he heard the sound of ripping paper.

"Sweetie, don't tear Daddy's book." (Hmmm, no, he couldn't reach her while driving.)
No reaction, just the sound of paper calmly, slowly being torn.

"Daddy needs that book. Don't tear Daddy's book." (Spoken with a little more authority in his voice.)
She ignored him and kept up her slow destruction of the book.

Then my words flashed into his mind – "Don't tell them what NOT to do. Tell them what TO do."

"See the pictures. See the pictures in the book? Look at the pictures. Look at the pictures in the book."

The ripping stopped. Matt's little two-year-old daughter was looking at the pictures, and slowly turning the pages.

How is this possible? How did that work? Why did it make such a difference? What could possibly be going on inside that cute little head? Is it possible that we have misjudged and misunderstood two year olds?

This book is full of many other insights and helpful tips like this that are just as easy to put into action. You can actually have fun trying them out. Test them; find out for yourself if it will work for you and for your two year old. And then maybe soon you too will be able to say: "They laughed when they saw me softly whisper a simple instruction to my naughty two year old, until they saw what happened next!"

Table of Contents

1 Twoness

Understanding two year olds is not something that came naturally to me, even though I was once a two year old myself! All I really know about that year is what my mother said, that at two, my only redeeming quality was how incredibly cute I was. I raised four daughters through that exasperating two-year-old stage of life, but it wasn't until after they grew up that I really developed a special interest in the phenomenon of two-year-oldness. You see, there was one year when all four of my girls had babies. So of course, two years later, I had four two-year-old grandchildren, and it was pandemonium whenever I visited any one of my daughters - or whenever they would visit us!

Since I'd had my own four two year olds one at a time, and life with them was such a challenge, I figured that I must be doing something wrong. But when I had four two-year-old grandchildren all at the same time, I began to revise my thinking. You see, each of my daughters is different (who would have known that opposite can go four directions – five, counting our daughter Sunny, adopted at age eleven). My four daughters covered all the bases: stay-at-home moms & working moms; experienced moms & new moms; and take-charge by-the-book or enjoy your kids / attachment parenting. It seemed like the one with the most experience had settled into following a very no-nonsense approach. The two first-time moms read lots of childcare books, and asked for our advice getting and applying all the input possible; the other experienced mom took the you-can-never-give-them-too-much-love approach of following her mothering instincts. My sons-in-law were even more different from one another. And the children themselves: three boys and one girl, are each so unique. But with all these differences, one thing remained the same: their kids all did that turning-the-household-upside-down thing. It really seemed to be natural, inborn behavior, not caused by anything outside the child. There was just something crazy about being two.

~

A few years after that, I was traveling with my daughter Sarah, who by then had four children of her own. We were in Austria sitting across the street from a sidewalk café where a family with five children was finishing lunch. Now in Austria having two children is considered to be a large family, so we were trying to figure out if this German speaking group was really one family, and not family and a few friends. The ages of the children seemed to be spaced like a family. We started with, how old does the biggest one seem – about twelve . . . just when Sarah said "and the little one is about two" the mother was lowering him into his stroller. As he firmly planted one foot on each arm rest and stiffened his legs, we said in unison: "Yes, he's two." And we also knew all too well the look of weary frustration on the mother's face.

In my travels I began watching for two year olds. In South Sudan in 2004 I noticed that no one seemed willing to stop two-year-olds from doing whatever they wanted. I remember watching children play one day, while we waited for the mothers to gather under the large mango tree where I was to teach a women's group; even the six year old let a two-year-old girl take away the "toy" he was playing with (a part of an old plastic container). In South Korea I was at an after-church lunch. Sitting near the pastor (a Korean man who had lived in the U.S. for a few years), we were both watching a cute little boy. I said to Pastor Kim, "In America the parents have a lot of trouble trying to control their two year olds. Are Korean two year olds as naughty as Americans?" He answered with a very serious tone: "Oh, they are much worse." Back in South Sudan a few years later, I was introduced to the adorable little daughter of a Sudanese man we worked with. Her mother seemed shy, but the little girl walked boldly up to us, curtsied, shook hands with us, and said, "How are you?" I later asked her father if she was three and to my amazement he replied that she was only two. When I said "Wow, she seems so well behaved for a two year old," he did what (apparently) any parent in the world would do after getting a compliment like that: he told me the story of her outrageous behavior on the day before.

All this is to let you know that you are not alone.
In fact, chances are your mother
could have told us stories about you, as well.

So, do not fear. Understanding what motivates two year olds and how they think will make a huge difference in your relationship with your little one. Not only will you have less frustration and enjoy life together more now, but understanding your two year old today can help you establish a great relationship based on love and respect, that will continue to bless their childhood - and your whole life together.

2 What Motivates Two Year Olds

Little babies are little bundles of potential, but so helpless. The amount of knowledge that must be learned just to get by in this world is so immense, it's impossible for us to grasp. For example: as adults we know all about the objects we see; just by looking, we can tell that an object is soft, rough, or smooth, but we learned to recognize these textures by experience. Luckily, we don't have to figure out how to teach these things to children. They *seem* to pick up this kind of knowledge automatically, but in reality they must teach it to themselves. So, all that touching of things they shouldn't and playing with things that aren't toys . . . is really their personal study program.

As soon as babies move from the womb into our world, their drive to learn is working (once they can get past the surprise of their whole new world, of course). It's fascinating to watch babies for signs of concentrated interest. How precious it is to hold a baby in the first moments of life and make eye contact – you will see the look. It's a look of deep concentration, fascination, and focus. You can almost see the little wheels spinning in their heads. This instinct to learn tends to rule their interests until they are about three years old. They have a LOT to learn!

New babies have very little control over their learning opportunities. We need to be aware that babies are really at our mercy when it comes to mental stimulation. It isn't until they learn to move their bodies that they can reach out, pick up, then crawl over to objects in their world. A toddler is a baby that can walk. A toddler's greatest delight is practicing all those new skills like walking and climbing to explore his world – especially if it's baby-safe. This phase can be tiring for parents. But life with a toddler is still mostly fun, and you can understand them – because you realize that they are still just babies.

Then, somewhere around their second birthday, your child is able to walk and run without thinking about how to run. Now the focus of interest shifts. They want to know everything about anything in their world. They become little scientists who must test the properties of the objects they find interesting. How does it feel, how heavy, how hard, what sound does it make if you hit it on the ground? What happens when you throw it, kick it, stomp on it, wash it, or flush it? You can still see the look of concentration, if you watch for it. They will try some of their experiments over and over. It is at this point (when a child has learned to control moving without having to pay attention to moving), where I feel that the stage they call the "terrible twos" begins.

It is amazing that children will pick up the language and culture where they live, while learning all about the unique part of the world they live in. If a newborn African baby girl was adopted by Austrians, she would grow up speaking German and have no idea how to carry water jugs on her head. Human beings have some truly instinctive behavior – those things that are the same for all people all over the world like the facial expressions that show happiness, sadness, surprise, anger, fear, and disgust. But most of what we do is not instinctive, we must learn how to do the things we do – and that is how it is that the amazing variety of lifestyles, cultures, and languages are possible.

I can't emphasize enough the incredible amount of things each of us needs to know, and so many of these things must be learned between the ages of two and three – so these little ones come equipped with a drive to learn. Their drive to learn is as real a drive as hunger or thirst. We understand many of our children's needs: food, shelter, a place to sleep, diaper changes, hugs, love, and so many other things necessary to their health and well being – and we provide them. But during and in between all those needs, is their need to learn. Their play is their work; it's how they learn. A child's compulsion to learn is essential for his survival. Two year olds are motivated by the need to learn.

3 How They Think

If you have a two year old in your life, then you already know that they don't think the way we do. So, how do they think? Well, the main issue is how they don't think - they don't think verbally.

Most of us begin to think in words around age three. True, they are talking now – using new words every day! But they don't have a large enough vocabulary or grasp of how words work together to think in words. (I'm not sure how a person can think without words. Are their thoughts mostly pictures and feelings?) So when you say "What is he thinking!?" you are asking a very good question.

A two year old might be able to say a lot of words and understand even more, and yet not understand sentences. I know a lot of Spanish words, but I am not fluent – and I certainly can't think in Spanish. When I spent two weeks in Nicaragua, a woman that I had been getting to know walked up to me after a meeting and told me something in a sentence ending with the words "no es muy bueno" and obviously wanted a response. Knowing I had to say something, and recognizing immediately the words "muy bueno" (very good), I responded "gracias" (thank you). As she walked off in a huff, I went through her words in my mind – I had recognized all of them but her sentence was just a little too long for me to understand instantly. I had to translate the words one by one into English before I realized, too late, what she was telling me: something I was personally in favor of was, in her opinion, "NOT very good." (I suppose that my odd response was probably about the best answer I could have come up with if I had known what she was saying!) Two year olds - no matter what language they are learning - speak it as a second language, and have to translate the words into whatever form their thoughts take.

Understanding that two's are not verbal thinkers helps your enjoyment of them in two main ways:

1. not making assumptions about their motives
2. communicating with them

Assumptions

With thoughts in forms such as pictures, touch, movement, sounds, and emotion you can imagine that decision making must take a very different path for them than it does for us! When anyone makes assumptions about the motives of a two-year-old, their guess may be WAY off. We make assumptions about their motives when we think "He knows I don't want him to do that, so he is doing that to defy me" or "To do what she just did, I would have to be really angry (depressed, afraid, hateful, wanting control, revengeful, uncaring, etc . . .)." You might imagine the same emotions that drive your actions are motivating your child, but consider this: even when you try to put yourself in your child's place by remembering what it's like to be a child, it's unlikely that your thinking can go back far enough, because nonverbal thinking is the main reason very few people can remember anything about their life before age three.

Communication

Knowing how to speak in a way that your child can understand will save so much frustration for both of you! This is such an important topic that one of my working titles for this book was, *How to Communicate with a Two Year Old.* Wise parents know it is vital to spend time chatting with, explaining things to, and reading to your little one. In fact there is probably nothing more important that you can do for your child's mental development.

But when you have something very important to communicate:

1) Speak slowly and clearly
2) Use simple words they know
3) Keep your sentences very short - two to four words
4) Repeat
5) Repeat using different words.

There is a lot more about this subject in the next chapter.

4 How to Communicate with a Two Year Old

People ask: "Why does my two year old do the opposite of what I say, and then throw a temper tantrum when I get upset about it?" It can be frustrating to be the parent of a two year old, but imagine how frustrating it must be to BE two. We know that they understand a lot of words, so we assume that they understand us when we talk. But two year olds do not think the way we do. We don't realize how abstract words like "no" and "don't" are. Twos have a very hard time trying to visualize or grasp negative words. Before we really get into what to do about it – I'm just going to illustrate the problem for you.

Years ago I saw a little cartoon with two panels. In the first, a woman is talking to her dog. The caption is "what you say / what your dog hears," with her word bubble "Now Rover don't do that. Bad Rover . . ." and the dog's thought bubble "blah blah Rover blah blah blah Rover . . ." The second panel's caption was "What you say / what your cat hears:" "Now Fluffy don't do that. Bad Fluffy. . . " with the cat's thought bubble: "blah blah blah blah blah . . ." Now I don't really want to compare my husband to a two year old, much less a cat or dog, but a couple weeks ago I asked him to pick up some green tea. I listed several brands that I like, then as he was going out the door I said "just don't get Lipton" (Sorry, but I find Lipton green tea to be bitter). Guess what kind of tea he brought back – sigh – do I sound like "blah blah green tea blah blah blah Lipton" to my well educated, caring husband, Dr. Dennis H. Janisse? So when we say to a two year old: "We are going into the store, don't run around and don't pick things up," what do they probably hear?

If you have ever tried to learn a foreign language, you are familiar with the process. You can study books, take classes, learn on the computer, even listen to it spoken and practice saying the words, but you can only go so far without spending time talking with people who speak it as their first language. When you start interacting, you listen to hear words you know and try to figure out what is being said, then search your mind for the right word to say. If the person you are talking with speaks too long or too fast you lose track of what is being said.

In applying this to a little child consider a sentence like "we are going into the library now so don't make a lot of noise and don't run." What would be the one word he'd remember first – you got it: "RUN." And he didn't hear the word "NO" at all (it was hidden in the word "don't"). My former friend in Nicaragua (Chapter 3) had no idea that I wasn't following her sentence, because we'd spoken enough that she knew I understood a lot of words. But apparently she hadn't taken note of how often I said "repito por favor" and " mas despasio" ("please repeat" and "more slowly," the most used phrases of those of us who don't yet think in the foreign language yet we are really trying to understand).

So we need to use two totally different ways of talking with a small child, in two different types of situations.

- normal speech for everyday conversations
- simple, clear speech for important information

How to Chit-chat with Twos

First let's look at normal everyday chit-chat. It feeds their drive to learn. Among the things a child is learning and developing as we talk with them are:

- language and how to talk
- a meaningful relationship with us
- how to interact with people
- knowledge about their world
- getting their brains ready for more complex thought.

In the book "The Mislabeled Child" parents are encouraged to "make sure your home is a rich and nurturing language environment" in order to prevent and to treat a variety of learning disorders involving language.[3]

Some examples of everyday speech and conversation are:

- listening to and answering their questions
- reading to them
- telling them stories
- teaching them poems and nursery rhymes
- telling them the names of things
- asking them questions

Most of the time we don't think about how we speak. But even in everyday conversation it is a good idea to think about it once in a while. So often when we speak, all the sounds that make up the words zip past the ears of small children so quickly that they have trouble separating the words within the sentence and telling similar sounding words apart. When you slow down and pronounce words very clearly as you discuss whatever the child is showing an interest in, he will listen to you, because you are making it easy for him to make sense of language.[4]

One wonderful way to enjoy little ones is to give them words and opportunities to use them. Most children hear a lot from television, but have little real back and forth conversation. Take the time to listen to them. Talk with two year olds about the things they are already interested in. Speak in complete sentences, with a full vocabulary of names of things, of action, and description. You don't need to use baby-talk yourself, but you don't really need to correct theirs. Listen patiently, and give them time to find the words themselves. Answer their questions simply; afterwards you can have a conversation about the subject. Ask them questions about things they have recently done or seen. Talk about some of the important things that can't be perceived with their senses, like our emotions: how helping, and hugs, and enjoying being together are ways of showing love, etc. Read to them, tell them nursery rhymes, teach them songs, and be willing to read the same book or the same poem, over and over. The fact that they are enjoying the repetition means it's fulfilling a learning need.

How to Communicate the Big Stuff

The second kind of talking with a two year old, is talking to communicate important information. There are times when it is essential that the child understand you. In order to keep them safe you must make warnings very clear. Other examples are when correcting their behavior, when teaching them a simple skill, or when they are having a tantrum. Here is what *you* need to know in order to successfully tell them what *they* need to know:

When it is very important that they understand you

1. Speak in very short sentences – two to five or six words at most (more with a calm older two – fewer with excited or younger children).
2. Use simple words – if possible, ones you've heard the child use.
3. Speak slowly and clearly.
4. Repeat exactly what you said, and also repeat using different words.
5. Tell him what to do, not just what not to do.
6. Make sure you have the little one's full attention. If possible talk to children before they get excited and distracted.
7. Keep the total conversation short.
8. Ask the child to repeat what you said. You may need to help with this.

Tell Them What to Do, Not Just What Not to Do

A negative sentence can be very confusing to a little one, so think of a way to put the information in the positive. For example,

rather than saying	Say
"Don't be so loud."	"Speak softly," or "Be quiet."
"Don't go in the street."	"Stay on the grass" or "Walk on the sidewalk."
"Don't pick the flowers."	"Just look at the flowers. Smell the flowers"

When you need to use a negative word or phrase, do it in a very clear way – contractions can make the sentence difficult for a two year old to follow.

Recently my two-year-old granddaughter, Marian, was visiting. As they were leaving Marian spotted my big bright orange daylilies and ran over to pick one to take home – I stayed right at her side.· Before she could touch them I engaged her in talking about the flowers (twos love to get the words to go with things they are interested in) "These big flowers are pretty!" "Do they have a smell?" We checked for fragrance and talked about the color. She reached out to pick it and I said (sadly) "No, no picking the big flowers. No picking grandma's big flowers. See these little flowers? You can pick them!" I showed her my honeysuckle vine. "Mmm, they smell so good." And I helped her pick some.

By the way, if you look you will find that almost any lawn has some little flowers growing in it – searching for them and picking them is a fun activity you can do with little ones. Even little clover leafs can be fun to collect. Help them find something fun that is okay to do.

Think of situations you have encountered in the past and try to imagine ways to give directions that are positive, short, and simple. They really need to know what they CAN do - not just what they are NOT allowed to do. After all, it might be easy to use words to *talk* about not doing something, but it's really hard to *visualize* or *feel* something that doesn't happen. Give them words that their little not-yet-verbal brains can use!

~

In the next chapter I'll talk about heading off tantrums before they start. But the reality of it is that tantrums can't be completely avoided. If your child is having a meltdown and you communicate with him in this way, it will not stop the behavior instantly. But it can help to begin the calming down process. Keep your communication as short as it can possibly be. Start by letting the little one know that you understand the source of his frustration, tell him what he cannot and can do, then ignore the bad behavior. This should shorten the whole process. The downside is that anyone watching will think you are crazy and ineffective – but you'll know the difference. The self-confidence and calm you project will surely impress any onlookers, including your spouse! If you can't control the child, at least you can control yourself.

5 Helping Them to Be Good

My daughter Heather is the mother of four boys and runs a licensed home day care. When I asked for her view of twos and their frustrations she wrote:

> *"I think people forget to baby two year olds because of all the changes that come with being Two. No more bottles/nursing, no more crib, no more being spoon fed, a lot less being carried around... on top of that two year olds WANT to do everything themselves. They want to open and close all the doors, throw away the diaper, hold the toothbrush (theirs and mom's), carry heavy things, and basically take over or imitate any task that mom or dad is doing. The combination of those two things seem to make adults forget that just months before they were thinking of and treating the 2 year old completely different. Adults try to anticipate a baby's hunger and sleep needs, and they hold, cuddle, talk to and "help" babies all day long. I notice a lot of parents trying to make the two year old communicate those needs all the time, instead of anticipating them, and just freely giving drinks, food, and down time."*

She summed up the predicament that two-year-olds find themselves in:

> *"Babies have all their needs anticipated and met - preschoolers can communicate clearly and in an acceptable manner - but poor two year olds aren't having all needs anticipated, and also can't communicate effectively."*

In other words, we bring a lot of unneeded frustration into the life of the child. They can do so much. So, outwardly we see them as capable, but inwardly they are still in many ways babylike. Just as teens in the transition from childhood to adulthood are not really adults or children, the two-year-old stage is the transition from baby to child. Maybe this has something to do with why parents generally find these two stages to be the most challenging.

Don't say "NO" unless you mean it!

I know - you want me to tell you how to control the child. But, I know two year olds, and I try not to expect more than they can deliver. I've seen parents whose thinking process seems to go something like this: "Okay! She can walk and talk – now I can treat her like a seven year old. I'll tell her what to do and make her obey." That's just not realistic. Obviously, there are times when the child must obey. So, I'll get right to the point. If you tell a child to do something, or not to do something – in the form of a direct command - be prepared to make it happen.

Not too long ago my grandson, Joseph, was playing with the buttons on the T.V. I told him to stop, but he didn't stop immediately, so I got up and moved him away from it if. It took a couple tries before we were able to get him interested in something else. It would be foolish to punish a two-year-old for this type of infraction.

Punishing a child for acting his age usually has unintended consequences, like:

- They learn to ignore the punishment because it becomes such a regular part of daily life.
- They may become confused, not connecting their action with your re-action.
- Constantly stopped from showing curiosity, they can lose their love of learning.
- You can lose your ability to be consistent.

Years before many of us knew anything about brain development, I would tell other parents to "just keep getting up and making them obey. Be consistent, and eventually they will figure out that if you say something, they will end up doing it, and they'll realize that they may as well obey on their own" and I always added: "they'll figure it out about the time they turn three." It is also clear that if you aren't consistent when they are two, they still won't do what you ask when they are three (or four, or five . . .).

If you say "no" more often than it is truly necessary then all this consistency can get real old real quick. Since you don't want to ever give up and just let the child do what you told him not to –

PICK YOUR BATTLES CAREFULLY.

- Before you give an order, ask yourself: "Am I willing to do whatever it takes to make sure this happens?"
- Have as few "no's" as possible.
- Ask yourself "what's it gonna hurt?" when deciding whether to create or remove rules.
- Focus on the serious issues.

Obviously it's hard to be consistent when you have lots of rules and lots of nos. On the subject of making rules for your kids, my husband says: "decide which mountain you want to die on" (he's also a retired US Air Force chief master sergeant). In other words, just as a company of soldiers shouldn't try to defend, or to take, territory that they are not ready to fight for to the end, you shouldn't start trying to get a child to do something that you aren't willing to carry though with no matter how much the child tries to resist. (Yes, this is a pretty radical example, but I really want to get through to you on this issue!) Oh, and the "pick your battles carefully" was one of my husband's sayings too.

We all know that:

- being consistent,
- following through, and
- doing what you say

are basics of child training, *but too many rules or no-nos make following through every time into an unrealistic goal.* <u>When you keep it simple, being consistent becomes possible.</u>

Giving commands and getting obedience

Often we need to get a child to stop what he is doing, put down what he's holding, change his behavior, or you are going someplace where certain behavior is required (quiet, walking only, keeping hands in pockets, holding your hand . . .) These are basic skills needed for guiding and directing two year olds:

1. Make sure they understand – keep your words clear and simple
2. Prepare children for change – the two minute warning
3. Redirection – help them move on to a different activity
4. Show them how to behave – be an example to follow
5. Breathe deeply and slowly, stay calm (I'm serious)

I'm a real believer in taking the time and trouble to PREVENT discipline problems. Do these things and you will be working with your child's nature, and not against it.

1. Make sure they understand: keep your words clear and simple

After you have done your best to tell them clearly what to do, ask them to tell you what you just said: "What will you do when I talk to the lady?" –"Sit. Read book." If your child can't tell you what you said – just do what language learners always ask for: repeat and speak more slowly. And once again, be sure to tell them what TO DO - rather than what NOT to do.

2. Prepare children for change: the two minute warning

Actually, it's more of a five minute warning: "We are going to leave soon. You can play five more minutes," followed in about five minutes by "We are leaving soon. Please help me pick up the toys – you can be my helper!" Better yet, give them something to help you carry out to the car. All too often, change surprises little children. They aren't expecting it, and they have trouble adjusting, so give them a little warning – four or five minutes is enough. If it doesn't work the first few times you try it, keep it up anyway – it may take time and experience for them to really see how it works (and how long minutes are). This little warning can save you from so many temper tantrums!

Charity's two year old, Mimi, had been playing in her wading pool long enough. But for Mimi it was never long enough! So Charity was not looking forward to the battle to get her out. She was one of the first to read this book and decided to try one of my suggestions by preparing Mimi for change with a five minute warning, and redirecting her with another activity. She announced that in five minutes it would be time to get out of the pool and get dressed to go in the car to Grandma's house. She asked her twelve year old to stay and watch Mimi for a few minutes while she got her purse. Returning to the backyard ready for the fight, she found Mimi out of the pool and towel dry, smiling and ready to get changed for the outing.

3. Redirection – help them move on to a different activity

One big key is to give them an alternate activity. When the child is doing something that (how can I put this) is a bad idea, begin by considering what it is that has captivated his interest then:

- think of something that might fulfill the same learning need,
- suggest it as though it is the most fun thing ever, and
- show them how it's done.

Heather was at an outdoor party with other young families. A little two-year-old boy had spotted the pebbles covering the pathway and garden border and was tossing them on to the grass. His mother kept pleading with him to stop, as she explained the damage rocks can cause to lawn mowers, but he kept tossing rocks into the lawn. So Heather got down on his level and formed a little pile of rocks in the path, saying "let's make some mountains!" He joined in and after a minute she went back to her conversation with the boy's mom, as he happily and harmlessly made little pebble hills.

When you give a two year old an alternate activity, then the child must choose to either fight you and stubbornly keep doing what he's doing, or give in to your suggestion. So be a person they can trust for fun. Like them, we also listen more carefully to some people than to others. If we think of someone as having good ideas, we will be more interested in what they have to say. To enjoy a two year old, you need to be the person they look to for help in following their drive to learn. It often helps if the activity is related to the one they are doing – it is much easier to make a small change in their behavior by giving them something to do that helps them satisfy their curiosity.

4. Show them how to behave – be an example to follow

The next chapter is all about how and why two year olds copy other people, and the amazing power of example. Notice how in the example above, Heather started doing what she wanted the little boy to do. Demonstrating exactly what you are asking them to do is such a great aid for the pre-verbal thinking style of twos.

5. Breathe slowly and deeply. Stay calm.

Be calm and confident. Confidence gives you an air of authority, and brings you respect.

Do Yourself a Favor - Simplify

Simplify your home a little. You can cut out so much stress and so many nos at home by putting easily damaged precious items out of reach, and better yet – out of sight.

Also, remember that those dangerous chemicals and sharp objects that you put out of reach when your little one was crawling and toddling around the house, may now be accessible to a resourceful two. Try to think and see your home through the eyes of a child who wants to see, touch, test, and generally play with everything possible. Get on your hands and knees and take a tour. Then do a little rearranging. Home should be a safe refuge for us all – with as few temptations, dangers, and conflicts as we can make it.

And then, when you are on the way to the house of someone with lots of breakable knickknacks, talk to them about the special way they must ask before touching anything there - and maybe give them a special little stuffed animal or other toy to hold, to help them keep their hands occupied in an acceptable way.

Why you may need to tell them ALMOST the same thing over and over

Two year olds can't generalize well. In other words, if a situation is not EXACTLY the same, they may not see it as being the same at all. Perhaps you taught your daughter not to walk too close to your swing set when another child is swinging and you see her always watching – then you go to the park and she walks right in front of the swing. It is a totally different swing set. To us it is obvious. To a two year old it may not occur to them that it is even similar. In the same way they may not realize that sharing their truck or crayons follows the same rules as sharing their candy or dinosaurs. Try to imagine how the world might look with their limitations, and be ready to carefully explain *almost* the same thing again and again.

6 Two Year Olds Watch Us, Then Copy Us

All day long we are using a powerful tool: EXAMPLE. Unfortunately we often use it mindlessly, enabling our little children to train themselves to do totally useless behaviors. Speaker and author, Gayle Erwin, is a dear friend. He tells about standing with his thumbs in his belt loops. He didn't even realize that he did that, until he noticed his little son studying him then carefully placing his thumbs into his own belt loops. [5]

To put the power of example to work for you, I want you to ask yourself two questions:

1. How can I model the things I want my child to do?
2. What naughty things might they have learned by watching?

How can you model the things you want them to do?

Think specifically. Imagine real actions you can do to model the behavior you want to see.

We have an amazing gift for training twos: they automatically copy us. They carefully study us and teach themselves to do amazing things that we could never teach them if we tried. Just watch the video on my website: 2-isms.com of the little boy playing his toy guitar next to his father. Could you imagine trying to teach a two year old how to act like a real guitar player by just *telling* him exactly how to hold the guitar, and describing in words strumming with a 'lost in the music' expression while swaying to the beat, but from time to time get a more serious look and adjust the knobs or keys . . ?

Once when my daughter Sarah was visiting my house, her phone rang. When she realized her phone had disappeared, she looked at Joseph (the little guitar player in the video) – in fact her husband and all the other kids also looked at Joseph. Sarah took the phone from him, read the message, and pressed buttons (while dodging Joseph's attempts to get it back). She gave the phone to Josh (the big guitar player). He texted an answer - while holding it over his head.

"He won't leave the cell phones alone!" they complained.

I asked Josh & Sarah "Do you know *why* he is so interested in it?"

"Uh, because it lights up and makes sounds?" they guessed.

"No."

" . . . It has buttons that really do things?"

"That helps, but it's not the main reason."

They stared at me and thought for a while.

"Because WE play with it?"

I smiled and nodded.

I didn't think they were convinced, so I spotted among the toys in my living room, one of the most visually boring items: a little bean bag my mother had made years ago. After I silently demonstrated examining it and squishing it, I tossed it to Sarah - who had just put the cell phone out of reach and out of sight, so Joseph still had his eyes on her. She played with it a little, doing a good job of looking totally fascinated, then she and Josh started tossing it back and forth. They ignored Joseph until he tried to get it, so they included him in the game of toss, until he walked away with it – studying it and feeling the little beans inside.

The brains of two year olds are designed to pay attention to what we do, and then give it a try. Think about it - they truly NEED to learn what people do with the things in their world - it's a huge part of their built-in drive to learn. They watch us, and then copy us. And they don't just watch *us*. I've been paying attention, and I'm convinced it's the main reason for that exasperating two-year-old behavior of: seeing another child playing with a toy then trying to take it. They obviously are not learning from their actions, since so often the result is crying, fighting, and getting scolded. Is he thinking: "I know there are lots of toys here, but I want to be mean and take a toy someone else has"? I think they are not thinking at all, just doing what they are driven to do – copy the people around them. (To know how to teach kindness, it helps to understand what motivates them.)

Heather, my daughter with the licensed home daycare, had purchased a cute child-size play kitchen. She showed it to the kids, but they ignored it. After a few days she had a flash. She just went over to it and pretended to cook at the stove, using the little pans, utensils and plastic & wooden foods. Without a word from her, kids came over to play and it soon became one of their favorite play areas.

So what are your goals? What do you want them to do that they aren't doing? How can you demonstrate, rather than only describe? Possible areas to consider using the power of example are:

• reading
• eating healthy foods
• turning off the TV when the show you wanted to see is over
• sharing with others
• dancing and singing
• saying "please" and "thank you"
• using the toilet (generally: father/son, Mother/daughter, son)
• washing your hands
• doing chores with a happy attitude
• saying "yes" to requests
• hanging the towel back up
• putting dirty clothes in the hamper
• enjoying the outdoors
• being kind to animals

You need to give thought to your goals for your child. Many of these things you already do all the time, and just need to make a point of letting your child see you do it.

What naughty things might they have learned by watching?

This second question probably requires some soul searching. You might have remembered seeing someone else, like an older child, set a bad example that started an undesirable pattern. It's hard to control the example others are setting, but maybe you can take this information and gently explain it to whomever it is who might be creating a problem. Now, the only person whose actions you or I can actually control is ourself, so it's important to think about the things we are doing, but it's so hard (and sometimes quite painful) to look at ourselves objectively. (Sometimes what we are doing is obvious to everyone but ourselves.) And yet this is where you really have power to change your little one. Try, as I have already suggested, staying very calm and speaking in a soft voice when your two year old throws a temper tantrum, and see if the fit is shorter than usual. If, like most people, you have been getting frustrated and showing it, then you might feel foolish if you *don't* react – after all this is serious; you should be upset! But stay cool anyway. Even if it doesn't help the child, it's great to have *someone* around who is calm when others panic – and it feels really powerful to be in control of yourself.

This is so important, in issues large and small. They *will* copy us. We need to be aware. Gayle Erwin also says "My wife and I worked really hard to teach our children good table manners, but it didn't work. They eat like me." Next time your child is doing something annoying, ask yourself – "Am I looking into a mirror, and seeing what my actions look like to others?" Don't be afraid. Take a very honest look at yourself. Self-knowledge is like the shot of Novocain before the doctor or dentist gets to work: sure it hurts, but it saves you from a lot more pain than it causes! So be honest with yourself and let your child teach you. Your little one might just be doing you a really big favor - by helping you become much more self-aware and a better person.

Controlling the examples in your child's life may mean that you restrict who your little one spends time with. You will also need to supervise closely, talk to family members, and choose childcare carefully. Even pay attention to characters on TV, DVD, et cetera.

It's so important to be open to changing some of the things you do and say. Maybe you will realize that you are doing that same thing that one of your parents always did *and you said you'd never do*! Here is a list of some of the problem areas that might spring from example:

- poor manners
- getting angry often or easily
- sloppiness
- impatience
- negativism
- ignoring others
- too much screen time
- laziness
- poor grammar
- using crude language (or worse)
- lying
- destructive behavior
- talking back and arguing
- poor eating habits
- teasing

Maybe it's just me, but arguing children is one thing that just drives me crazy. Not so much children arguing with each other – that's a natural activity that can help them learn how to work things out. I'm talking about adults and children arguing with each other. We've all seen two year olds who argue with their parents (and we all know that it takes at least two people to have an argument). I like the way my daughter Heather handles arguments with kids. She decides before she says "no" that it is something she will not change her mind about – wisely, she normally says yes unless there is a very clear reason to say no (not leaving herself any room to give in to argument). She is now able to stop her older boys quickly by saying "When Mom says 'no' does she ever change it to a 'yes'?" You have to have history backing you up for that to work!

"NO!"

Another common problem in twos is negativity. For many two year olds it seems that their favorite word is "NO!" But since I have been researching and studying two year olds, my daughters have really made a point of making sure that my two-year-old grandkids have lots of yeses in their lives, and not too many nos.   In focusing on their brain development - by allowing the natural learning drive to guide their child's activities, rather than focusing primarily on behavior training - it turns out that their behavior is being beautifully shaped by their love of copying us.

To explain what I mean, here is an example from something my daughter Sarah did.   A couple months before this writing Sarah decided to spend a few days saying "yes" to every reasonable request her children made (she's homeschooling her eight children ages thirteen to two).

Sarah wrote on a Facebook post:

> *"For the past three days I didn't tell my kids what to do. I tried to say "YES" to ALL their ideas and requests. I made an effort to supply them with whatever supplies they needed for any project.   Then I followed them around and took pictures. They kept quite busy... And they only asked for my help a few times."*

Looking at the pictures she took that day I can just imagine:

"Mommy, can I color with markers?" - "Yes!"

"Can we play Monopoly?" – "Yes!"

 "Can I look at your coins from other countries?"

"Can we mix baking soda and vinegar and watch it fizz?"

"Can I bake a cake and make it look like a castle?"

– "Yes, yes and yes!"

She kind of ended up with a habit of just saying "yes" to her kids a lot.   Her two-year-old son got used to hearing Mom say "yes" immediately after he asked for something (anything *reasonable*, of course), and he began copying her by quickly saying "yes" and then doing what he is asked. *Who would have thought?!*

Not always, but often, habits, good and bad, get started by following someone's example. It is sad to think that a child is making himself and others miserable by doing what comes naturally: copying other people. A two year old just doesn't have the ability to reason why something is okay for someone else to do, but wrong for him. How good it is when this natural ability results in a more charming and happier child. The power of example is not a magic wand, but sometimes it seems like it!

7 Twos Find Everyday Chores Exciting, If They Get to Help

It's so wonderful that *two year olds have a natural desire to help out.* Instead of plopping your youngster in front of Nick Jr or Sesame Street so you can get your housework done, enlist him as your helper. I know. I know. I know. It is SO much easier to do the work yourself. But what about when your child is seven, and is a willing, skilled, and experienced helper? – all because you took the trouble to train him when he naturally wanted to help. Of course, this book isn't primarily about the future – it's about surviving and enjoying life now. The better future part is just a happy side effect.

This book is about understanding the natural motivations of two year olds, and working with their nature so that both adult and child can enjoy life more. Their desire to help out can be a wonderful asset – it has little to do with getting the chore done, and everything to do with your child's development, learning, and happiness.

Try to not divide your life into categories: this is when I clean the house, this is when I exercise, this is when I do yard work, when I cook, when I go shopping, when I have quality time with my offspring. . . Your little one shouldn't be an item on your to-do list. Find ways to safely include your two year old into as many daily activities as possible.

There are so many wonderful benefits of letting your child help with chores. Your little helper will:

- have fun
- learn practical skills
- learn to enjoy the satisfying feeling of completing a "job well done"
- practice following a series of steps
- feel that he has a valuable purpose in life (I'm not kidding – this is basic to happiness for anyone)
- spend meaningful quality time with you
- keep alive his love of helping others
- be closely supervised while you work (which could save you a lot of time later when you clean all your cosmetics out of the bedroom carpet – Elmo can't always be counted on to captivate.)

HOW you recruit his help is important

Don't just say "Clear off the table," say "Help me clear the table." And it's not "Go get the broom" it's "I'm going to sweep the floor. Come and help me." "You can be my helper" and "I need your help" are exciting phrases to two year olds. Before you call them, have a plan. Know what part you want them to do. Show them what to do and work together: telling them in simple words and short sentences each step of the job – one step at a time. This is especially important with new tasks. And give them feedback. Tell them when they are doing well, and help when they start to slip up. Have fun. Let them see everyday activities as something to enjoy, and let them know you enjoy doing things with them.

More than once I've been visiting a friend or relative and have seen the two year old run excitedly to get the little child-size broom the moment mommy starts to sweep. And mom always looked so proud! Working together doesn't necessarily mean that the child has to do real work. In the days when most clothes would wrinkle (except for polyester leisure suits), I had a friend who gave her daughter a toy ironing board set. They would do their ironing together. The little girl would "iron" her doll clothes and they would chat like grownup ladies. It was so cute. She said she had fond memories of "ironing" beside her mother. Personally, I usually found ways to avoid ironing altogether.

Here are a few ideas for ways your little one can be a helper:
- Put something in the trash for you.
- Bring you something.
- Help set and clear the table.
- Put clothes in the hamper and hang up towels after a bath.
- Wipe up spills.
- At stores, put items into the cart & take them out at check out.
- Help water plants (outdoors, unless you want to risk root-rot from stealth overwatering).
- Help feed animals.
- Take scraps out to the chicken coop or the compost pile.
- Help stir pancake or muffin batter.
- Press pause on the DVD.
- Pick strawberries or tomatoes.
- Put flowers in a vase.
- Wipe off a table.
- Hold the dust pan for you.
- Help carry things in from the car especially "big" or "heavy" things.

Just remember, with a two year old, you are working together. You might be able to hand a stack of napkins to your five year old and find one next to each plate at the table, but with a two - I wouldn't count on it. You might just find them used as teddy bear blankets or clogging the toilet. Give the napkins to your little one when you take out the plates and silverware - and supervise. *Pushing a child into any activity they aren't ready for usually takes the fun out of it; and the last thing you need to add to your two's life is extra stress and frustration!* Keep chores as a fun activity that he will look forward to. You may even want to phrase the call to help as an optional request "Would you like to help Mommy?" This way there will be no argument. It's the child's own choice to make, so it is a win/win situation: they say "yes" and you get to spend quality time together in a practical educational activity, or they say "no" and you can get the chore done without all the hassle of their help.

8 Eating, Sleeping & Potty

I was not planning to include a chapter on these three subjects in my book. These kinds of things aren't really what this book is all about. Not only are there a lot of books on these three subjects, but each family also has its own approach. My goal is simply to help people to enjoy two year olds. Then my daughter Sarah came to visit for eleven days and brought her two year old (and her seven other children, age four to thirteen). I realized that a few insights on these subjects might just help make life with your two year old more enjoyable, because eating, sleeping and potty are three essential functions that every human body will do. Growing from babyhood to childhood means going from following nature to following the way it's done where we live.

I would love to just tell you what to do. It would be so much simpler to simply say "Do it my way." If I were to do that it would be something like this:

Eating:
Eat three healthy meals around the table as a family every day & keep only nutritious foods available for snacks.

Sleeping:
Have the same bedtime and bedtime routine every night: bath, saying good night to all, bedtime story, lights out, prayer, hug, & kiss.

Potty:
Wait till they seem to be ready and then make a big deal of buying panties or underwear, and have a jar of m&ms to reward "going."

Okay, now that I got that out of my system, let's get on to the real world.

By real world I mean that you have to figure out and decide what will fit your family, your life, and what you will actually do. To help you figure that out, I'll just give a few basic principles.

<u>Eating</u>

When I was about thirty-five I started putting on about a pound a year – except when I would diet, when I would lose a few pounds and then always put it back on with an extra pound or two. After a few years, it was adding up. At age thirty I wore a size five, by fifty my size twelve jeans were too tight! And for obvious reasons I had become afraid to diet. I didn't know what I was going to do! Then I heard of a simple eating plan where you

1. **only eat when you are hungry;**
2. **stop when you are full;**
3. **eat what you are in the mood for.**

I kept these rules diligently and within a year I was slim again. And have been ever since. As an avid two year old watcher, I have noticed that twos keep these rules quite naturally.

When we make a big deal over eating, we can train our kids to ignore their bodies and overeat. I'm not saying that you should just leave food out where they can reach it and let them fend for themselves. I am saying that you should be sensitive to their appetite levels and let it guide you into helping them be hungry at mealtimes, and comfortably satisfied in between. Twos have little bodies that require very little food to power, except during growth spurts when they may need a lot of nutritious food. When they are in the process of adding a half an inch of height in one month, they may eat everything you put in front of them and ask for more. In between growth spurts three peas, a chicken wing, a tablespoon of potatoes, and half a glass of milk might just satisfy. Dish them up a small amount and give them more when they have eaten it all and now want seconds. If you give them more than they are able to eat, remember that teaching children to overeat (by requiring them to "clear their plate") won't do anything to help the starving children in Africa.

Eating together as a family will make it easier for you to teach a child not only healthy eating, but table manners as well. The children will see you eating things and usually their natural way of copying might be all the encouragement they need.

Be aware - most kids have a built in aversion to anything that looks like leaves or mushrooms, has a strong flavor, or even looks unfamiliar. This really is a good thing because it tends to keep them from eating poisonous items outdoors. In some children this is a really strong force, but other children will eat anything. This picky phase usually passes, so take it easy and don't force-feed the kids. Offer a wide variety of foods. Introduce new foods gently, and keep offering the foods they don't like. I always required my children to at least taste it or eat a little tiny piece of everything. And always keep available those nutritious foods that they DO like.

Obviously, it is much easier to get children to eat properly and at mealtime if they aren't eating junk food all day. And it's easy to keep them away from empty calorie foods if the cupboards aren't filled with it. I know some people who keep junk food for themselves to eat – it's easier if you have something you like you don't have to fix and that won't rot if it sits around for a week – and then they try to keep their kids from eating too much of it. On the other hand, I also know families where the parents have become very heath conscious *but* don't want to deprive their kids of the stuff they love to eat. If either of these families describes you, *please, don't act like there is something wrong with your child because they won't eat dinner.* And really think about what you want to have in your house, and maybe even make some changes.

Some examples of very nutritious foods that many 2 year olds like:

- apples
- bananas
- oranges
- strawberries
- carrots
- cucumbers
- broccoli
- cheese
- yogurt
- grapes
- raisins
- scrambled eggs
- peanut butter on celery or apples

(sunflower seed, or almond butters, too)

__Bedtime__

Okay, I am a grandma, and though I don't feel like a "senior citizen" I do qualify for the discount at some places. I have discovered that falling asleep isn't always as automatic as it used to be. If I don't keep a few simple rules I've made for myself, and follow my "bedtime routine" - I may find myself lying awake tossing and turning. In fact, though of course I keep *my* complaints to myself, I can relate to my two-year-old grandson's whining and crying over being put to bed when he can't fall asleep. Here are a few rules that I keep. You can figure out how to apply this to two year olds.

Bedtime Rules for Senior Citizens
(Also work quite nicely for toddlers and anyone else)

No screen time (TV or Computer) just before bed
No aerobics or jogging before bed
No major argument (especially unresolved) before bed
No caffeine after 5:00 pm, and not much after lunch
Eat a light snack so I'll be neither hungry nor full
Neat, quiet, dark room
& comfortable bedding and nightclothes

(A child might like a night-light, some white noise [a fan] or soft instrumental music, a book read to them, and should not have caffeinated drinks at all - it has a much stronger effect on their little bodies, and some researchers believe that too much can interfere with the development of a child's nervous system.)

Typical Bedtime Routine for Seniors
(You probably have a bedtime routine of your own!)

Check locks & stove, turn down the furnace (open a window, set the a/c a little cooler) turn out some lights, brush teeth, take a relaxing shower, apply night creams, then read pleasant nonfiction until drowsy.

A bedtime routine signals our body that it's time to shut down for the night. I don't know about you, but I can't just tell myself to sleep – I have to let myself go to sleep. Falling asleep isn't just a decision we make – like staying awake might be.

A routine also is calming in several ways:

- It provides a predictable pattern – it's nice to know what will happen next.
- It gives us a little time between stimulating activities like play and TV, before we are lying in bed trying to sleep.
- It gives rules that parents can use to calmly and confidently say: "No, you had a snack and drink before bed," or "No, we just do one story and one song" (or four stories and five songs . . . much more than that and you lose track).
- It is enjoyable and so the child will be able to become calm and ready to sleep.

If your child's bedtime is a nightly nightmare – even before anyone in the house is asleep – and you decide to try a bedtime routine, don't expect it to work well the first night. After all, *if it has only happened once it isn't a routine yet.* You will want to tweak the pattern for a couple nights until you get it just right for your family. Then once you have been sticking to it for a few days, your little one should get used to the pattern and begin to respond. I know that it seems easier to just pop them into bed with a video on. You are exhausted already from caring for them, on top of all the other commitments you have, but you all will get more rest if bedtime actually results in a child calmly falling asleep. So make the choice now to find the energy to establish a pattern and stick to it. Sweet dreams.

At the beginning of this chapter I mentioned Sarah staying with us. She had come to visit because her husband was going on a business trip – and coincidentally my husband was traveling also. She had morning sickness and getting her eight children to bed without her husband's help was the one thing she just didn't handle well. While tucking in the little ones upstairs, her "big kids" age nine to thirteen downstairs would either tease each other and get into arguments, or would join forces and get into trouble!

Since it was my house, and Sarah freely admitted to not knowing what to do, I felt free to go beyond just meddling to actually taking charge! I established a bedtime routine the first night. The TV and all other electronics were off for a half hour before bed. We did calm activities like reading or having real conversations. Then we started with baths for the little ones, followed by a serving of yogurt to eat at the table.

They brushed their teeth, said each goodnight to everyone, and I watched the older kids while their mom tucked them in with a couple stories and prayer, then lights out. It went okay – just a little getting up to whine, tattletale, or ask for drinks of water, and they eventually went to sleep.

Within a few days we had tweaked the routine to fit the family. For example, we dropped the baths – with that many kids it took too long and beside, half of them had gotten so dirty during the day that they had to get baths earlier. The kids, including the two year old, got used to the routine and within just a few days, once they were tucked in – they didn't get up again until morning. (Which came much earlier that we hope it would!)

<u>Potty</u>

Sigmund Freud and Erick Erickson's theories about two year olds (actually 18 months to three years) have been rejected or at least modified by many experts on child development. From the late 19th century to the 1950's they popularized their theories that, for two year olds, the primary drive is to be in charge (autonomy) and potty training is focus of this developmental stage. These theories still influence attitudes toward two year olds today!

My first real learning about twos started in 1968 when as a student nurse I first studied child development. At that time we were told that two-year-old children have discovered that they can control things and will try to control everything and everyone in their lives. I was also taught that they are very negative and will say "NO!" as a part of their basic nature. Those areas that the child can control (the subjects of this chapter) must be handled very delicately or you will produce a warped adult with all kinds of neuroses. But then a few years later when I had a toddler of my own, the message of those around me was: "If your child is still in diapers after eighteen months of age, you are a lousy mother!" Thankfully, from my point of view, since the popularity of disposable diapers, neither mother nor the child is usually motivated enough to worry about it until the little one is around two years old. And my opinion of Freud's theory – well, I don't think it was ever the *child* who focused life around potty training.

Each child, and each mother is different. Find an approach that you are comfortable with. If it doesn't work, give the child a couple weeks off and try again – with a different approach, or the same one. During that time your child will probably be paying attention to what it feels like to need to go.

<u>Here are a few signs of readiness you can see in a child:</u>

- awareness of the need to go
- understands and uses words related to going potty
- ability to help with getting dressed

Of course you can help your little one learn these things. In fact "The Baby Whisperer" says for two weeks before you begin potty training you should take the poopy diapers (cloth or disposable) and let your child watch as you dump the "poo" into the toilet – where it is supposed to go.[6] Doing this can help you avoid the situation described in the next story. This was about a little girl – but boys can have the same problem.

I was once babysitting a two year old for a few days. She was no longer in diapers – except for night time. And there was another exception: she would ask for a diaper to 'poop.' Afterward I took the diaper and dumped its contents into the toilet saying "This is where poo is supposed to go." But I got an argument from this cute little child. "No. Mommy always puts it in the trash." So I said "Well, I'll be sure to tell Mommy that it belongs in the toilet." The next time the child needed to poop, she sneaked into the bathroom and tried out letting the poo go directly in to the toilet for herself. Being so proud of the accomplishment, she had me come and see her achievement. Naturally, I was totally delighted and very proud of her too. Her mom was delighted too, and it hasn't been a problem since.

Often daycare providers (or grandmothers, your older sister, or an experienced friend) have experience with great methods that really work. Their insights can often be really helpful. They may even offer to potty train your child for you! If you trust their patience and wisdom, and they are willing – great. Be sure to ask them what you should do to help prepare the child and how to follow up.

If you don't already have a plan, here's a simple way to start:

- Buy a potty chair or toddler seat for the toilet.
- Let your child come into the bathroom with older siblings, a friend who is close to their age, or parent (usually of the same sex) and they should say things like, "Grownups wear underwear and go potty in the toilet. I don't wear diapers."

- Watch a really good video together that teaches potty training and/or read them children's books on the subject.
- Go together and buy underwear (at least eight pairs and loose enough for the child to pull down and up easily).
- Ask your little one: "Would you like to start wearing panties/underwear like Mommy/Daddy and Lilly/Conner?" et cetera.

You can also:

- Find a how-to book on the subject and follow the plan.
- Use the book ***Toilet Training in Less Than a Day*** [7] – and follow the method in every detail: make the lists, practice with the doll, plan a whole morning when just the two of you are at home alone, and buy the favorite drinks and snacks as suggested. (I have used it several times - and it really worked!)

While your child is new to being diaper free:

- Remind the child from time to time by praising your child for wearing dry panties/underwear.
- And/or remind the child from time to time by asking her if her panties are still dry or if she needs to go potty.
- When necessary, sit in the bathroom with your little one.
- As much as possible let your child wear just a shirt or short dress with underwear at home, or be ready to assist with the clothes, for a while.
- Consider using small pieces of candy or other special treat reward.
- If you are quite sure he must need to go, it may be a good idea to give a reminder when the child is in the middle of an engrossing activity.

- Decide the level of firmness or permissiveness you want to use, but don't yell or punish – this usually just makes them fear the process and slows it down.
- Remember, when there are changes in life – new baby, move, illness, travel – it is pretty normal for a two year old to have accidents.

There are some things in life that you just can't control, and these three areas are among them. It is your two year old who is in control of his own body. You can guide and encourage, but it is up to your child to follow through. The goal is to help the child to move from babyhood to childhood. Keep in mind that you can make children sit at the table, but you can't make them eat. You can make them get in bed, but you can't even force *yourself* to sleep. You can get them to wear underpants and sit on the potty, but only they have control over when and where they go. The plan is to get them to want to. It is much easier for all if you can find ways to work with their basic nature.

Twos want to do what other people do, they are good at copying, they like to be helpers, they like to know what's coming next, they want to learn all about their world, and they want to do things by themselves. If you can find creative ways to use these traits to guide their behavior, your job will be much easier.

9 What to Do About Tantrums

Temper tantrums, meltdowns, and conniption fits, whatever you call it – this is the point when your adorable little sweetie "has lost it." Screaming, crying, throwing themselves on to the ground, clenched fists, and kicking feet are pretty standard. But some children have their own personal tantrum style. From our perspective it can feel like an attempt to hold us hostage to their will: "Do what I want or you know what will happen!" But the reality is clear – the child is not only out of control: he's lost control. How can we control them if they can't control themselves?

My approach to discipline is to focus on preventing bad behavior. So this chapter is not exactly a plan for dealing with problems. But since bad behavior will happen, this chapter has some basic principles, and a few specific tips. I have found that most people have pretty strong feelings about child discipline and will do what they feel is best for their family. I've already talked about staying calm, so I hope I don't have to remind you not to let anger drive your responses to your little one.

Avoiding Temper Tantrums

The best way to handle a tantrum is to avoid it all together. Think back to what triggered meltdowns in the past, and plan to prevent the frustration that so easily overwhelms twos.

We already talked about smoothly changing activities. For some children, stopping them in the middle of their play can be traumatic.

As an artist, I know the frustration of being "in the zone" working on a painting – and being interrupted. I've learned to be polite about it. But sometimes the flow is lost and I have a sense that the painting that was developing will never be quite what it could have been. It seems that it feels the same way for a small child in the moment of being told to stop now.

Two year olds take their work (which is of course what their play really is) just as seriously! We need to help them with the change. Give them a warning – a little time to finish what they are doing and mentally prepare to do something else. If the "something else" is something they don't want to do – a more fun little activity in between might ease the change. Some activities naturally come to an end by themselves, like carrying something big or heavy back to the car (house, bedroom . . .), racing or marching to get there, getting a drink of water, or being your helper. So when this new task is complete you won't need to deal with ending the fun once again!

Another major tantrum trigger begins when your child asks for something that you do not want him to have. This is *not* an issue like making them eat what you serve for dinner; it is something that you can actually control. They are at your mercy and they know it. It is a big mistake to ignore their request, or even to just say "no." If you do that, children will usually try harder to convince you how much they want it, how important it is to them, what a great idea it is. Their frustration level rises because they are sure that if you just listened and understood you would get it for them or let them do it. But if you keep ignoring, saying no, and telling a child why you won't buy the item/allow the activity, without first acknowledging their point of view, there will usually be a meltdown.

We all have seen older children do this as a ploy to get what they want, but tantrums in a two (especially a young two) are usually caused by overwhelming frustration. So, take action before anyone is upset.

Right at The Beginning – In the Early Whining Stage :

1. Listen to the request.
2. Tell them you know they really, really want it.
3. Confidently (not with irritation – sound like you really care) say "no."
4. If they still argue, do step 2 & 3 again.
5. If you want to give a reason for your denial, keep it simple, short, and honest. (Note: saying "I can't afford it" makes no sense to a two year old.)

Try this and you will be amazed by how much the child wants to know that you listen and you care – maybe even more than he wants the thing that was so important. This pattern of responding actually even works with teenagers and just about anyone else too!

Responding to Tantrums

But what about those times when you are not able to prevent a tantrum? It will happen. In the chapter on communication I talked about how to speak to a child having a meltdown. The simple, clear communication will not stop the tantrum – but it will help begin the calm-down process. Your goal should be to help the child become calm – *without doing something that will encourage future temper tantrums*. Don't give them what they are crying for. If it is something that you want to give them, it's best to wait until the child is calm. Usually the real cause is an overload of frustration, and your goal is to help your little one learn to handle frustration, and become more patient. Demonstrate calmness. And, there is nothing wrong with completely ignoring them while they melt down, as long as you stay close by.

Press their Reset Button

In the height of a meltdown, a two year old might not be able to really hear or see or understand anything. But there comes a point where the child is able to take in a little input from you. Now is the time to "press their re-set button." When you have your hair dryer on high for too long, it gets overheated, and it turns itself off, then you have to let it cool down for a while and then you must press the little red button in – the reset button - before you can turn it back on. When the little one is beginning to calm, sometimes they get stuck in just crying or repeating some action or words – try a total change of subject, attitude, and action: "Oh my goodness!! I totally forgot that I wanted to check and see if there were any roly-poly bugs under the rocks in the backyard!" Use your imagination.

Correction

The most difficult area of discipline is when correction is required. Issues like: hurting another child, and putting himself in danger – *after being told specifically not to*. Stern disapproval and a no-nonsense time out, are the common first options, but always look for a way to "make the punishment fit the crime." Examples are: clean up the mess, the toy is put up, the activity is ended, if he hurts another child, it's time to stop playing together. Make sure you clearly and simply explain the connection between the act and the punishment, whatever form of correction you use.

Remember the goal of discipline is to change future behavior.

I also feel strongly that one of the most important things you can teach a child is honesty, so, if the child told me what really happened, and the only way I knew about a bad action was the child's confession - I won't give the child a harsh punishment. If a punishment "fits the crime" the child will usually see it as fair, and be more apt to learn from the experience.

Each child is unique. Some are naturally compliant, but it is possible that most of the more typical two year olds – stubborn, self-willed, and noncompliant – have such an intense drive to learn that it is very hard for them to see a greater value in obeying you, anyone, or anything else. You've probably heard the commercial tag line: "Obey your thirst." Well, that's what the two year old does – obeys the thirst for learning.

Negativity

We all know that temper tantrums are much more likely when your child is hungry, thirsty, or sleepy. A child that is not allowed, or provided with, learning opportunities is hungry too – hungry to learn. It's sad, but it is common, for a two year old to get very negative:

saying "no" to any suggestion, saying "no" to other kids, and just walking around saying "no" – over and over. So, as I already said, give your child as few no's as you can; really think about what your rules will be and make your home child-friendly.

Enable your little one to feed the need to discover, experience, and investigate. Learn to enjoy the noise children make when they are playing happily. Don't let yourself be irritated by their constant motion. Give them opportunities to "get their wiggles out." Spend time outside with them every day that the weather permits – and it doesn't have to be perfect weather. Or at least, put on some music and get them dancing. The very best discipline is preventative.

Creating new habits

It's important to be aware of how habits start. We don't want tantrums to become a bad habit now, do we: the danger of giving in after the child cries long and hard. Every behavior creates a pathway in the brain that makes it easier to do it again. It is a scientific fact that the more you do something, the more natural it is for you to do it again.[8] So by guiding your child into activities where he behaves well, you help him build habits of being pleasant to be around.

10 Having Fun with Two Year Olds

Small children have a very short attention span – at least that's what we've heard. And when we try to hold their attention, we often find this to seem so true. And yet when they get involved in activities like the ones listed in this chapter, they are often able to focus intently for quite a while. Maybe what is called "attention span" is just the amount of time they are able to focus on what someone else wants them to do – rather than on what their inner drive to learn is telling them to focus on. Maybe the need to learn is so great that they naturally possess a very low tolerance for boredom. Their brain is telling them that what they are being asked to do is not something they need to learn right now – their learning drive is directing them to a different "educational opportunity" by telling them "Hey, it would be really fun to play with that thing over there instead!"

And so, for me one of the more frustrating things about two year olds can be: never being sure that they will be interested in what I want them to do. I can have fun ideas, but the child is disinterested. We *cannot possibly* design a curriculum to teach toddlers and two's all they need to learn, or to know exactly when they need to learn it, but the great thing is, their brain will provide the curriculum. *All we have to do is aid the child in their quest for all the actions, encounters, information, and experiences that they are intuitively seeking.* So when I am going to spend time with a two year old I arm myself with a variety of fun things to do – both items to play with together and things for the child to play with alone – and I go with the flow. Then I try to keep all my expectations pretty general, and we are sure to have fun. Let me help you visualize this.

Last year, when I first began to work on this book, I 'babysat" five of my grandchildren. The two middle girls – three & five played together, first doing arts and crafts, putting my Old English Sheepdog on a leash and taking him for walks inside the house, then playing house with little stuffed animals. The nine-year-old girl played with the baby, made snacks, chatted with me, and made a little art project. The baby crawled around in my baby-proof living room, stopping to play with baby toys I put out, and when he got bored I showed his big sister how to teach him to put blocks in and out of a clear, plastic wide-mouth jar I'd cleaned & taken the labels off of for this very purpose. After that he took a nap. Then there was two-year-old Laura.

Laura started with the blocks. After that, snacks. Then Laura wanted to paint, so I set her up with watercolors and she discovered (that with recently used paint) you can scoop globs of thick paint out with the brush and she was getting as much on herself as on the paper. So, trying not to interrupt her creativity I cleaned her up a little (wet paper towel or baby wipes work fine for this). I always get the washable watercolor sets at a very low price when school supplies are on sale at the end of summer. She saw her sister using the child scissors, but since she is still not ready for those, I gave her the more harmless kids zigzag scissors and watched as she cut strips of construction paper into little bits, for a while. And I made sure the scissors were left at the table. She then went and found the three little stuffed animal horses she had brought and got three of my throw pillows and put them on the floor in a corner of the dining room. They were my older

& dark colored pillows and the floor was clean so I didn't have to redirect her into anything more appropriate, she made beds for the little horses. A big sister and baby brother came to join in the fun. Then she moved on to making my sheepdog into a bed for herself. The only time she was upset happened after her mom arrived and I wasn't watching her so closely: she started teasing the dog by making "raspberry" sounds, until he barked and jumped, frightening her. I never had to get to my almost-never-fail toys: sandbox or water play in the back yard.

We all had so much fun, but clearly it was a pretty frenzied time – but what were my options: make her do what her sisters are doing or what I want her to do? Try to force her to be happy with each activity for longer periods of time? If my granddaughter visits me by herself, I try reading, singing, or taking a walk with her, but when twos can see other children - all the movement and sounds get their attention and they lose focus, so each activity ends up being pretty short. When I know I'll have several kids at once, I plan possible activities before they arrive and then hover over them with my full attention while they are here. When we love and enjoy the children in our lives, the "hovering" can be a lot of fun!

With just one child you can just say, "Let's go look at my books. You can tell me which one to read." To a two year old this can sound like exploring and making choices: activities they are usually ready for anytime – except, perhaps, when they are excited, distracted, hungry, tired or sick.

Play Time Ideas

Alone or Together

Playing together is great and I talk about that in the next section, but it is also important for a child to have time to "work" undisturbed. We can give them some input to help them get started, then enjoy a break (kind of a break – you still need to keep your eye on them) as they:

- *work on skills*

- *experiment to discover the properties of things in their world*

- *enjoy examining things*

- *investigate*

Don't force undisturbed play; just make it an inviting option, in a quiet place where they won't be disturbed or too distracted. When they do focus all their attention on a task or examining something, they will get that expression of complete absorption (just like when they were babies). It's at times like this that their developing brains take the information they have been gathering and make new connections.

Work on Skills:

Here are some examples of activities that you can help your child be able to attend to without interruption. If you do them together just remember to not do too much of the work yourself.

- zipping, snapping, buttoning, using velcro
- turning pages, opening and closing things
- eating a snack with a spoon or fork
- building with blocks, or other stacking toys
- dressing themselves, or their toy animals or dolls
- coloring, drawing, painting, paper tearing, play dough, mud pies
- balance and movement skills like hopping, jumping, climbing, dancing
- throwing, rolling, bouncing balls

These are the kinds of skills that, after a simple demonstration, the child can work on by himself. There is no series of steps or complex procedure to follow. For that kind of skill, the two of you need to work together. These are the kinds of skills that a person just has to get the feel for. As you supervise for the safety of the child, there is usually no need to interrupt their focus, but when you do give praise, encourage and praise their hard work and accomplishments.

Experiment and Discovery:

These experiments are ideal for solitary play and don't require much direction, though they generally require some supervision *(the larger the amount of water, the more carefully you must pay attention to their safety)*. You provide the opportunity - all they have to do is play.

- pouring water from container to container
- making musical sounds – instruments for kids like xylophone, flute, harmonica, drum, guitar, tuning forks
- a pan, sink, or little tub of water and: floating items, funnel, sponge, soap . . . (don't leave them alone)
- sand, mulch, pebbles, gravel, snow, dirt, mud (you may draw the line where you wish)
- playing with shadows, a prism, flashlight

Your little scientist is very good at finding his own experiments too; if it is safe and harmless be sure to let him enjoy his research project.

Examining and investigation:

These can be done alone, *while supervised for safety* - both for the item and the child. They are wonderful things to do together too!

- books, albums, catalogs
- plants, flowers, weeds,
- rocks, shells,
- pinecones, seedpod, acorns
- watching harmless insects like ladybugs, roly-poly bugs, and caterpillars

Playing Together:

Expand their collection of ideas for play

It's great for you to do things together that will open the child's mind to new games, new ways to play, new areas to investigate or skills to work on. These are great ideas to suggest to babysitters and mothers helpers, too.

Make believe play

Make believe play can be based on real places they know about, like playing house, store, and restaurant; places and things they've never seen like a visit to Africa, Antarctica, space travel, and sailing on the ocean; or fantasy like being a magical princess or transforming into a robot. Remember games you liked to play, imagine new ones, or get an idea from them and run with it.

Sarah wanted her daughter Anna to keep the two youngest children in the family busy for a couple hours while she worked on a project in the kitchen. Since, like most eleven year olds, Anna often loses focus when watching her little brother and sister, Sarah knew that she needed more direction. I had given Sarah a printout of this chapter to proofread for me, so she gave it to Anna. She showed her the section titled "Show How to Pretend" and told her to do some of these things with the kids. They had fun for hours combining "Play with Stuffed Animals" and "Roll Playing" activities.

Playing with trucks and cars
> *They already know how to race and crash!*

- going on a trip
- delivering things
- creating a little city using blocks, boxes, sand, etc.

Play with dolls or stuffed animals
- Make a zoo with the stuffed animals then have the dolls visit.
- Be a lifeguard, fireman, policeman, or superhero who protects and saves the action figures.
- Create a pretend family.
- Be a pilot, bus driver, train conductor, or captain of a ship - with stuffed animal passengers (perhaps their bed can be the vehicle, or you can build one from pillows).
- Have a tea party.
- Pretend they are doing all the things the child does each day (you can go through the whole day from waking up to getting tucked in).
- Have them put on a show (it can be a way to get a shy child singing – after all it's just the teddy bear singing the song).

Role Playing

Make believe with dress-up costumes made from:

- ties
- scarves
- towels
- fabric

- briefcase or purse
- hats
- bathrobe
- your clothes

Costume Box – you can collect items from thrift stores, garage sales or your own closet – including props and accessories.

You can become:

- royalty
- pirates
- rock stars
- animals

- firefighters
- astronauts
- explorers
- dancers . . .

Role playing is also a great way to
Teach children how to act in different situations
by pretending you are going places and doing things such as:

- a restaurant
- a kids party
- a formal tea party
- going to the store
- the library
- a museum
- going to school or church
- hiking in the woods
- the dentist or doctor
- a wedding
- going to the movies (you can take tickets, make popcorn, darken the room, and then watch a short video).

Playing with real things

Two year olds love their toys, but they also love to play with real things. Your house is full of perfectly safe items that a child can play with:

- A cardboard box – depending on the size – can become a jewelry box, treasure chest, car, boat, or a house . . . Get an appliance box from a store that sells stoves and refrigerators, cut a door and windows in it and give your two year old crayons or markers to decorate their little house inside and out.

- Pots and pans and wooden spoons make fun drum sets, or for pretending to cook.

- Empty paper towel rolls can be used as musical instruments, a spyglass to look through, or for sword fighting. And look for other potential toys in your recycle bin.

- Indoor water play: lay out a towel on the floor (wood, tile or vinyl – not carpeted) put a jellyroll pan, cookie sheet, or cutting board in the middle of the towel and give your child a variety of small plastic, metal, wood cups, bowls, scoops and spoons and a cup full of water.

- Blankets or sheets can turn chairs or a table into a playhouse, a cave, fort, or a tent.

- Pillows and blankets can become a nest or a boat.

Making Something Together

When you make something together you not only create something real, but you create a wonderful memory, and sometimes a keepsake that will remind the child of the time you spent together having fun. Here are some ideas:

- simple arts and crafts – where they can do most of the work themselves
- stringing beads to make bracelets (watch extra closely)
- find a roly-poly bug under a rock, put it in a jar, collect thing for it to climb on – and watch it together. Lady bugs and grasshoppers are great too, but harder to find.
- baking a cake, making cookies
- plant a garden or just a few beans in a jar
- pick flowers and put them in a vase together (if you have a tiny vase you can search for flowers in the grass)
- My daughter Charity's two year old, Marian, had drawn so many colorful pictures that they taped them up to create her own little art gallery and posted pictures of it on Facebook.
- Make a photo album

Making a little photo album can create a special treasure. Many children don't really get to look at pictures of their family, relatives, and themselves – except for a quick look at the back of the digital camera right after you take it. Your photos are in the computer. It's easy to get some printed at the drug store, and buy a little photo album there too – the kind with one photo to a page. You can show your little one how to put the pictures into the plastic sleeve, as you talk together about the people in the pictures. They are so proud of themselves when they show it someone, both for making it and for being able to name the people and talk about the pictures. They can take it with them if they are spending the night away from home, and you might just find your little one quietly looking through it.

For some children, drawing or painting can become a time to "work on skills" more than a time for creating art work. I was visiting my daughter Heather when her two-year-old son had just become very interested in drawing circles. If we ever needed to change his activity all we had to do was invite him to sit in his highchair and color. He made page after page of little and big circles and spirals. Outside he would use sidewalk chalk to draw circles everywhere. One day, when he was coloring, I sat beside him and drew pictures too. I didn't say, "I'm going to teach you to draw faces." An older child would love to hear that, but Carsten had just turned two so I just started to slowly draw, as he watched. First I carefully made a circle like the ones he was doing, then I added a curved line and two tiny circles, and suddenly the circle had become a happy-face! He watched spellbound as I drew a few more. After that he began adding random lines and tiny circles to his pictures. A couple weeks after I returned home Heather emailed me pictures of Carsten's latest drawings: pages filled with colorful happy-faces!

Made-up Games

Sarah made up a game. Little Joseph learned nursery rhymes and little poems as she read them over and over. Then they play *Say The Missing Word*: "Hickory, dickory, _____. The mouse ran up the

_____." He loves it. And he's so proud of himself! Once it's really easy for him, she makes it a little harder – until he is saying almost every other word.

They also make up stories. Joseph holds his hand like a little open book then has Mom start reading, leaving out words for Joseph to fill in to make the story his own. For example,

Mom: "One day Joseph looked out the window and saw _____."

Joseph: "A fire truck!"

Mom: "The fire truck was _____"

Two-year-old Joseph actually invented this game!

Charity and Marian (Mimi) play "*Magic Rocket Ship*." Mimi gets under a blanket, they count down, make rocket sounds, and then when they land Mimi opens the rocket door (throws off the blanket) and Charity says "Wow, we've landed at _____ !" then Mimi announces the destination and off they go around the house playing *visiting the children's museum* or *the zoo . . .*

I like to play *Changing from Caterpillar to Butterfly* with my grandkids. After crawling around being a hungry caterpillar my grandchild wraps up in a blanket (taking a large colorful scarf) then pops out as a butterfly dancing and running around with fluttering silk wings!

When I was little we played games that even a two year old might enjoy. Try having the child leave the room and then hide a small object in plain sight – and see if they can find it. It's kind of like Where's Waldo – harder than it sounds - you have to give hints – "you're getting warmer."

You might remember games you played as a child that are simple enough to teach a two year old. You can make up new games of your own. Get ideas for games on the internet. Follow your child's lead and make up a new game together. Or just play traditional games like hide and seek.

Two year olds love singing motion songs – like The Wheels on the Bus, learning sign language, dancing, and action nursery rhymes like "This is the Way the Ladies Ride" and "This Little Piggy Went to Market."

Do your exercise workout with them. Teach them yoga moves. Put on music and do aerobics – or just dance!

Playing Outdoors

Have you ever heard or said "use your indoor voice," or "don't run in the house?" There is great freedom in playing outdoors. There are things you can do outside that may not be allowed inside like:

- jump
- yell
- throw and kick a ball
- run around
- play with sand, water, leaves
- blow bubbles
- learn how to roll down hill

Kids need to do things like these! They need to be in a variety of environments for their proper development. They need to run around on sloping and uneven ground, not just perfectly flat floors. They need to be in open areas where they can see things that are a mile away, not just flat walls fifteen feet away.

The outdoors has so many interesting shapes, surfaces, and sizes for them to see and touch. Investigate the rough tree bark, hard rock, shapes of leaves and colors of flowers. Teach them to wonder at clouds, sunsets, tall trees, flying birds, the wind, and the moon. Children don't always notice these things automatically. Once when my daughters were children I pointed out a rainbow when a friend was with them. She was about ten years old and she said it was the first rainbow she had ever seen. I was shocked – how sad. Imagine all the rainbows she missed just because she wasn't looking for them.

Water!

There are so many ways kids can play with water outside on a warm day. Some possibilities are:

- a dish pan full of water and cups, a funnel, and bowls; toy boats; help them find things that float or sink; wash rocks or anything washable
- an empty shampoo bottle full of water to squirt
- a spray bottle full of water
- a big paint brush and bucket of water to paint the concrete, fence, walls, rocks…
- water the plants
- make mud pies
- learn to pour water from plastic bottles and pitchers to cups
- squirt guns
- and of course – the hose, sprinkler, or a shallow wading pool

Once again, remember: the more water the more closely you watch

Games

There are so many games that you can *only* play outside

- shadow tag – trying to step on the other person's shadow without letting them step on yours
- any other game of tag (like "freeze-tag")
- catch (start with rolling the ball)
- races – running, hopping, rolling . . .
- ring-around-the-rosy, London bridge (to two year olds nothing is corny or uncool)

Clearly exercise is good for all of us and really important for children's developing bodies. *But there are also some immediate benefits from letting little ones play outside.* After all that free play and exercise they will:

- be calmer indoors
- sleep so much better at night.

As I noted before, the weather doesn't have to be perfect for outdoor play. Of course lightning and high winds are a safety issue, and extreme heat and cold, or wet (when it's cold), might be a health issue. In hot weather always give them plenty of water to drink. But I never let just the fact that "it's nicer in the air conditioning" be a reason to keep them inside all day.

If you don't have a yard, go to a park or just take a walk. Taking a walk together should be a special time to share. In my work I get to do a lot of people watching, (sitting around at art shows waiting to sell a painting) and more than once I've seen a little girl trying to show some delightful discovery to her mother who is talking on a cell phone, ignoring her completely. It breaks my heart. So, when you are there – be there. Talk about what you see, or what you did yesterday. Search together for rocks one day, then notice every flower the next. Of course your child will want to have input, and you may end up spending weeks collecting leaves every time you step outside together – but that's okay. And if you must take a cell phone call, do just what you would do if you were with an important adult: ask to be excused for a moment, then keep the call short.

Screen Time

TV, video games, and computers are to playing & learning, what candy is to eating. The kids love it and so we let them do it. But wise adults limit the amount. If kids are eating candy, then they won't have an appetite for more nutritious real food. In the same way, if kids are watching a video, they are not playing with real objects or with a real person. If you give the child a choice between a lollipop and an apple, they'll take the candy almost every time. And if a kid's show is on the TV, they'll usually watch it. [9]

Toys

Some of the best toys have lots of different uses – like blocks or a wagon. They allow children to use their imagination. Some of the best toys don't cost much - like balls, little plastic farm or zoo animals, and toy cars. And at garage sales you can often find good quality toys which the youngest child in a family has outgrown. It's great to have a swing set or something to climb on, but nothing beats a sandbox!

Toys that challenge the mind and help a child be creative can be great for working together or for the child to do alone – if the toy is not beyond their abilities. The idea is to have fun, not frustration.

Remember: learning what they need to learn now will be enjoyable for them. But if a creativity toy is difficult for your little one - work together on it. Examples of creative and learning toys are: puzzles, dress-up dolls, sticker books, coloring, play-dough, lacing cards, and painting.

Fun with visiting two year olds

Before a two-year-old visits your home, get down and take a look at your place from their perspective. Crawl around and see if there are dangers or temptations that you need to remove, hide, watch the child around, or limit access to that area. Twos can learn that they must behave differently in different places – so tell them if you have any rules that are different from home. But keep the no-nos to a minimum, and you'll both be more relaxed.

Think of some ways to entertain your little guest. You may not have toys, but if necessary you could get out plastic bowls and cups, maybe you have some sturdy and harmless things made of wood, and if you can take the noise, let them play with your pots and pans. They love drawing with ballpoint pens and pencils on copy paper. If you have no children's books, consider looking at any books with pictures, photo albums, or pick some up at the library. Ask the children's librarian for books that are good to read aloud to two year olds – and they will show you some really fun books. But keep in mind that tearing paper and drawing on any flat surface available is also something many twos like to do, so be sure to enjoy the books together. They can enjoy board books alone, if you keep all writing implements out of sight, and out of reach.) Be sure to think up a variety of activities. When the little one arrives, *get down on the floor, and enjoy the adventure.*

11 Enjoying Two Year Olds

When I first had children I read everything I could on raising children. The popular theory at the time was that the phenomenon known as the terrible twos is caused by a child's awakening awareness of their ability to control things. (I know that from an adult perspective there are a lot of reasons to make this assumption.)   There were basically two approaches to the issue and both were ineffective if your goal was to enjoy your two year old. The permissive "never say 'no' method" was generally rejected by parents, knowing that two year olds really do need lots of guidance from adults. The other reasoning was that the child needed parents to be in charge – set limits, make rules, and enforce them. We were told that their desire for "autonomy" must be controlled - and so the battle begins: who will be in charge of the family life?!

I believe that if you see your job in raising and caring for a two year old as a battle for control, then your approach will actually become self-fulfilling: if you are always standing in the way of your child's opportunities to learn, then that necessary learning drive will force him to fight you for every possible learning opportunity he can get. Or even more sadly, sometimes a little one may just give up and begin to lose the love of learning. It may be that imposing this battle for control upon your relationship can drive a wedge between parent and child that sets the tone for life.

On the other hand, I have seen and experienced how watching for little ones to show an interest in something, then helping him to see, or touch or hear the object of his interest - just like we do for babies - sets a tone of caring. When we love someone, we listen, we pay attention, we are concerned about them, and we want to meet their needs. Loving someone means we enjoy being together. The bond between the child and parent or grandparent, caregiver or friend, can just grow stronger with time. Trust develops as the adult does not battle a child who is simply following an intense and indispensable drive to learn. The adult needs to give guidance. Sometimes it means saying, then enforcing, "no," but more often the best kind of correction is turning the child's attention away from dangerous or challenging behavior into a more appropriate activity. Raising a well behaved child is a good thing, and so is raising a happy child – a confident child who gets along with others, loves learning, and reaches his potential.

Heather has said of each of her boys when they were two: "It's a good thing he's so cute!" I believe there is an important reason why two year olds are so cute – so we'd naturally have tender and merciful hearts toward them. Sometimes you just can't help smiling at the crazy things they do. In fact, there are times when I am with one of my daughters that we have to avoid looking at each other, in order to keep from bursting out laughing at the hilarious antics of her naughty two year old. A tender heart and a sense of humor really help make it possible to enjoy two year olds!

Raising two year olds is a lot of work. Just being with them takes a commitment of time and energy, but that doesn't mean it can't be fun! A two year old is a non-verbal thinker who is motivated by an irresistible drive to learn. They cannot think like us yet and they cannot deny their urge to study, discover, and teach themselves everything they need to know and do and to be in order to survive and thrive in their world.

As I write this, those four grandchildren that got me started on my quest to understand two year olds, Samuel, Isaac, Ryan and Jillian, are thirteen years old – they've become teenagers! Isaac and Ryan have two-year-old brothers now, and Jillian has a two-year-old little sister! My daughters have learned so much about two year olds – and we've taught each other a lot over the years. They have been a wonderful resource for writing this book. Now, when I visit one of these daughters' homes, or they visit me – their two year olds create so much fun. What a difference from eleven years ago. I think Marian, Joseph, and Carsten are three of the happiest people I know!

Two year olds are amazing little creatures! Soon they'll learn to
think with words and to reason through their decisions;
their brains won't be so desperate for input;
and they won't need you in quite the same way -

SO ENJOY THEM WHILE YOU CAN!

Resources and References

Chapter 2

1. J. Ronald Lally. *The Science and Psychology of Infant-toddler Care*. www.zerotothree.org. 2003. Is a great resource for more information on this topic.

2. Joan Beck. *How to Raise a Brighter Child*. Pocket Books. New York. 1999. Is a great resource for more information on this topic.

Chapter 4

3. Brock Eide, M.D., M.A., and Fernette Eide, M.D. *The Mislabeled Child*. Hyperion. New York. 2006. (p172)

4. *The Mislabeled Child.* The authors explain that children will learn more easily and do better in school if the adults in their lives have been speaking with them in clear rich language. Babies and young children love to listen. Their little brains are busy filing away words, fitting together the structure of the language.

Chapter 6

5. Gayle Erwin. http://www.servant.org/

Chapter 8

6. Tracy Hogg. Melinda Blau. *Potty Training: Top Tips From the Baby Whisperer*. Simon & Shuster. New York. 2005.

7. Nathan Azrin. *Toilet Training in Less Than A Day*. Pocket Books. 1989. The original version of this book, which I used, was written in the 1970's.

Chapter 9

8. MaLesa Breeding. Dana Hood. Jerry Whitworth. *Let All the Children Come to Me.* Cook Communications Ministries. Colorado Springs, CO. 2006. (Page 108)

Chapter 10

9. Jill Stamm, Ph.D. *Bright from the Start.* Gotham books. New York. 2007.

Printed in Poland
by Amazon Fulfillment
Poland Sp. z o.o., Wrocław